SELF-MASTERY PUBLICATION

369

Manifestation

& AFFIRMATION

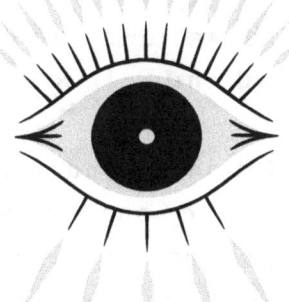

this book belongs to

_____

WHY THIS
method works

A positive affirmation is a statement **telling your subconscious mind about a reality**. Your subconscious does not know the difference between the reality you affirm and one that is real.

So, positive affirmations can reprogram your subconscious mind and help bring desires to life.

The 3-6-9 Manifestation Method provides structure to this process. Repeating your affirmations 3 times in the morning, 6 times in the afternoon and 9 times before bed can be truly transformational.

The specific use of 3, 6 and 9 in this process is attributed to famous inventor Nikola Tesla and his research. This concept was explored further by Karin Yee, who combined Tesla's number theory with the work of Law of Attraction expert Abraham Hicks.

Through **positive affirmations** and **structured repetition with these divine numbers**, you can manifest your desires and transform your life.

HOW TO
use this journal

BRAINSTORM
Define your goals.

The process of brainstorming helps you define your true goals. The best goals are measurable and include an emotional motive.

WRITE IT DOWN

1) Define Your Goals
2) Create Your Affirmations
3) Repeat Affirmations Daily

EXAMPLE GOALS:
I want to earn $100k a year because it will help me feel successful. It will give me financial freedom and allow me to take my family on epic vacations, which will bring joy into our lives.

EXAMPLE AFFIRMATIONS:
I am successful. Money flows as easily to me as air flows into my lungs. I am worthy and capable of making $100k a year.

REPEAT AFFIRMATIONS

morning (x3) | afternoon (x6) | before bed (x9)

DEFINE YOUR GOALS
brainstorming

To begin, take a deep breath and feel deeply grateful.
What are you grateful for right now?

___

What do you desire to manifest? Be specific.

___

Pretend you already have this desire.
Imagine your new life. How is life better, different or special?

___

How does it feel like to have your desire?
What specific emotions does it give you?

___

FORM YOUR
affirmations

Start writing affirmations for your goal. Avoid using negative words. Use positive words that support your goal and the positive feelings that come with it.

Examples: I am worthy of success. Money flows towards me. Success comes easily to me.

_____
_____
_____
_____
_____
_____
_____
_____
_____
_____
_____
_____
_____
_____
_____
_____
_____
_____
_____
_____

Choose your favorite affirmations. Now on the next pages, repeat x3 in the morning, x6 in the afternoon and x9 at night before bed. Repeat this process for at least 30 days to see how your life transforms.

morning - 3   Date: /   /

1.

2.

3.

afternoon - 6

1.

2.

3.

4.

5.

6.

evening - 9   Date: /   /

1.

2.

3.

4.

5.

6.

7.

8.

9.

I am the master of my own destiny.
I am worthy of what I desire.

morning - 3   Date: /   /

1.

2.

3.

afternoon - 6

1.

2.

3.

4.

5.

6.

evening - 9   Date: /   /

1.

2.

3.

4.

5.

6.

7.

8.

9.

My reality is a product of my thoughts and actions.
I deserve to have what I want.

morning - 3

Date: /   /

1.

2.

3.

afternoon - 6

1.

2.

3.

4.

5.

6.

evening - 9   Date: /   /

1.

2.

3.

4.

5.

6.

7.

8.

9.

I am the architect of my life.
What I desire is within my reach.

morning - 3   Date: /   /

1.

2.

3.

afternoon - 6

1.

2.

3.

4.

5.

6.

evening - 9   Date: /   /

1.

2.

3.

4.

5.

6.

7.

8.

9.

My beliefs shape the world around me.
I am capable of receiving my desires.

morning - 3   Date: /   /

1.

2.

3.

afternoon - 6

1.

2.

3.

4.

5.

6.

evening - 9   Date: /   /

1.

2.

3.

4.

5.

6.

7.

8.

9.

I am the author of my own story.
I have the right to receive what I desire.

morning - 3

Date: /   /

1.

2.

3.

afternoon - 6

1.

2.

3.

4.

5.

6.

evening - 9   Date: /   /

1.

2.

3.

4.

5.

6.

7.

8.

9.

My thoughts create my reality.
I am deserving of all that I seek.

morning - 3   Date: /   /

1.

2.

3.

afternoon - 6

1.

2.

3.

4.

5.

6.

evening - 9   Date: /   /

1.

2.

3.

4.

5.

6.

7.

8.

9.

I am the sculptor of my own life.
My desires are in alignment with my highest good.

morning - 3   Date: /   /

1.

2.

3.

afternoon - 6

1.

2.

3.

4.

5.

6.

evening - 9   Date: /   /

1.

2.

3.

4.

5.

6.

7.

8.

9.

My intentions manifest my reality.
I am open to receiving all that I deserve.

morning - 3   Date: /   /

1.

2.

3.

afternoon - 6

1.

2.

3.

4.

5.

6.

evening - 9   Date: /   /

1.

2.

3.

4.

5.

6.

7.

8.

9.

I am the captain of my own ship.
The universe supports me in receiving what I desire.

morning - 3   Date: /   /

1.

2.

3.

afternoon - 6

1.

2.

3.

4.

5.

6.

evening - 9   Date: /   /

1.

2.

3.

4.

5.

6.

7.

8.

9.

My reality is a reflection of my inner world.
I am worthy of abundance and prosperity.

morning - 3   Date: /   /

1.

2.

3.

afternoon - 6

1.

2.

3.

4.

5.

6.

evening - 9

Date: / /

1.
2.
3.
4.
5.
6.
7.
8.
9.

I am the painter of my own canvas.
I deserve to live a life of joy and fulfillment.

morning - 3   Date: /   /

1.

2.

3.

afternoon - 6

1.

2.

3.

4.

5.

6.

evening - 9   Date: /   /

1.

2.

3.

4.

5.

6.

7.

8.

9.

My consciousness creates my reality.
I am deserving of all the good things in life.

morning - 3   Date: /   /

1.

2.

3.

afternoon - 6

1.

2.

3.

4.

5.

6.

evening - 9   Date: /   /

1.

2.

3.

4.

5.

6.

7.

8.

9.

I hold the power to shape my own future.
What I desire is already on its way to me.

morning - 3   Date: /   /

1.

2.

3.

afternoon - 6

1.

2.

3.

4.

5.

6.

evening - 9   Date: /   /

1.

2.

3.

4.

5.

6.

7.

8.

9.

My mindset shapes my experiences.
I am worthy of receiving my heart's desires.

morning - 3   Date: /   /

1.

2.

3.

afternoon - 6

1.

2.

3.

4.

5.

6.

evening - 9   Date: /   /

1.

2.

3.

4.

5.

6.

7.

8.

9.

I am the director of my life.
I am open to receiving everything that I deserve.

morning - 3   Date: /   /

1.

2.

3.

afternoon - 6

1.

2.

3.

4.

5.

6.

evening - 9   Date: /   /

1.

2.

3.

4.

5.

6.

7.

8.

9.

My energy influences my reality.
The universe conspires to bring me what I desire.

morning - 3   Date: /   /

1.

2.

3.

afternoon - 6

1.

2.

3.

4.

5.

6.

evening - 9   Date: /   /

1.

2.

3.

4.

5.

6.

7.

8.

9.

I am the creator of my own fate.
My desires are valid and important.

morning - 3

Date: / /

1.

2.

3.

afternoon - 6

1.

2.

3.

4.

5.

6.

evening - 9   Date: / /

1.

2.

3.

4.

5.

6.

7.

8.

9.

I am responsible for the world I experience.
I am deserving of love, success, and happiness.

morning - 3   Date: /   /

1.

2.

3.

afternoon - 6

1.

2.

3.

4.

5.

6.

evening - 9   Date: /   /

1.

2.

3.

4.

5.

6.

7.

8.

9.

My thoughts determine my reality.
I am worthy of the life I desire to create.

morning - 3   Date: /   /

1.

2.

3.

afternoon - 6

1.

2.

3.

4.

5.

6.

evening - 9   Date: /   /

1.

2.

3.

4.

5.

6.

7.

8.

9.

I am the driver of my own life.
What I desire is already mine, I just need to claim it.

morning - 3   Date: /   /

1.

2.

3.

afternoon - 6

1.

2.

3.

4.

5.

6.

evening - 9   Date: / /

1.

2.

3.

4.

5.

6.

7.

8.

9.

My perspective shapes my reality.
I am deserving of a life filled with abundance and
joy.

morning - 3   Date: /   /

1.

2.

3.

afternoon - 6

1.

2.

3.

4.

5.

6.

evening - 9   Date: /   /

1.

2.

3.

4.

5.

6.

7.

8.

9.

I am the owner of my own destiny.
My desires are a reflection of my highest self.

morning - 3   Date: /   /

1.

2.

3.

afternoon - 6

1.

2.

3.

4.

5.

6.

evening - 9   Date: / /

1.

2.

3.

4.

5.

6.

7.

8.

9.

My actions create my reality.
I deserve to have my dreams come true.

morning - 3

Date: /   /

1.

2.

3.

afternoon - 6

1.

2.

3.

4.

5.

6.

evening - 9   Date: /   /

1.

2.

3.

4.

5.

6.

7.

8.

9.

I am the ruler of my own universe.
I am worthy of all the blessings that come my way.

morning - 3   Date: /   /

1.

2.

3.

afternoon - 6

1.

2.

3.

4.

5.

6.

evening - 9   Date: /   /

1.

2.

3.

4.

5.

6.

7.

8.

9.

My attitude determines my reality.
I deserve to be happy and fulfilled.

morning - 3

Date: / /

1.

2.

3.

afternoon - 6

1.

2.

3.

4.

5.

6.

evening - 9   Date: /   /

1.

2.

3.

4.

5.

6.

7.

8.

9.

I am the master of my own universe.
What I desire is in alignment with my soul's purpose.

morning - 3   Date: /   /

1.

2.

3.

afternoon - 6

1.

2.

3.

4.

5.

6.

evening - 9   Date: /   /

1.

2.

3.

4.

5.

6.

7.

8.

9.

My mind shapes my reality.
I am worthy of all the good things that life has to offer.

morning - 3   Date: /   /

1.

2.

3.

afternoon - 6

1.

2.

3.

4.

5.

6.

evening - 9   Date: /   /

1.

2.

3.

4.

5.

6.

7.

8.

9.

I am the designer of my own life.
I deserve to live a life of peace and prosperity.

morning - 3   Date: /   /

1.

2.

3.

afternoon - 6

1.

2.

3.

4.

5.

6.

evening - 9   Date: /   /

1.

2.

3.

4.

5.

6.

7.

8.

9.

My choices create my reality.
My desires are a reflection of my truest self.

morning - 3   Date: /   /

1.

2.

3.

afternoon - 6

1.

2.

3.

4.

5.

6.

evening - 9   Date: /   /

1.

2.

3.

4.

5.

6.

7.

8.

9.

I am the captain of my own fate.
I am open to receiving all that I am worthy of.

morning - 3   Date: /   /

1.

2.

3.

afternoon - 6

1.

2.

3.

4.

5.

6.

evening - 9   Date: /   /

1.

2.

3.

4.

5.

6.

7.

8.

9.

My reality is a reflection of my beliefs.
I deserve to be treated with kindness and respect.

morning - 3   Date: /   /

1.

2.

3.

afternoon - 6

1.

2.

3.

4.

5.

6.

evening - 9   Date: / /

1.

2.

3.

4.

5.

6.

7.

8.

9.

I am the conductor of my own life.
What I desire is within my power to manifest.

morning - 3   Date: /   /

1.

2.

3.

afternoon - 6

1.

2.

3.

4.

5.

6.

evening - 9   Date: /   /

1.

2.

3.

4.

5.

6.

7.

8.

9.

My reality is a reflection of my energy.
I am deserving of a life filled with purpose and meaning.

morning - 3   Date: /   /

1.

2.

3.

afternoon - 6

1.

2.

3.

4.

5.

6.

evening - 9

Date: / /

1.

2.

3.

4.

5.

6.

7.

8.

9.

I am the generator of my own experiences.
I am worthy of receiving all the good that life has to offer.

morning - 3   Date: /   /

1.

2.

3.

afternoon - 6

1.

2.

3.

4.

5.

6.

evening - 9   Date: /   /

1.

2.

3.

4.

5.

6.

7.

8.

9.

My thoughts and feelings shape my reality.
My desires are a reflection of my deepest desires.

morning - 3   Date: /   /

1.

2.

3.

afternoon - 6

1.

2.

3.

4.

5.

6.

evening - 9   Date: /   /

1.

2.

3.

4.

5.

6.

7.

8.

9.

I am the navigator of my own life journey.
I deserve to live a life of abundance and wealth.

morning - 3   Date: /   /

1.

2.

3.

afternoon - 6

1.

2.

3.

4.

5.

6.

evening - 9   Date: /   /

1.

2.

3.

4.

5.

6.

7.

8.

9.

My reality is a projection of my consciousness.
What I desire is meant for me and no one else.

morning - 3   Date: /   /

1.

2.

3.

afternoon - 6

1.

2.

3.

4.

5.

6.

evening - 9   Date: /   /

1.

2.

3.

4.

5.

6.

7.

8.

9.

I am the author of my own experience.
I am worthy of all the opportunities that come my way.

morning - 3   Date: /   /

1.

2.

3.

afternoon - 6

1.

2.

3.

4.

5.

6.

evening - 9   Date: / /

1.

2.

3.

4.

5.

6.

7.

8.

9.

My life is a reflection of my beliefs and values.
I deserve to be surrounded by love and positivity.

morning - 3   Date: /   /

1.

2.

3.

afternoon - 6

1.

2.

3.

4.

5.

6.

evening - 9   Date: /   /

1.

2.

3.

4.

5.

6.

7.

8.

9.

I am the creator of my own happiness.
My desires are a manifestation of my highest potential.

morning - 3   Date: /   /

1.

2.

3.

afternoon - 6

1.

2.

3.

4.

5.

6.

evening - 9   Date: /   /

1.

2.

3.

4.

5.

6.

7.

8.

9.

My thoughts and emotions create my reality.
I am deserving of a life that is filled with love and laughter.

morning - 3   Date: /   /

1.

2.

3.

afternoon - 6

1.

2.

3.

4.

5.

6.

evening - 9   Date: /   /

1.

2.

3.

4.

5.

6.

7.

8.

9.

I am the master of my own thoughts.
I am worthy of experiencing all the beauty that life
has to offer.

morning - 3   Date: /   /

1.

2.

3.

afternoon - 6

1.

2.

3.

4.

5.

6.

evening - 9   Date: /   /

1.

2.

3.

4.

5.

6.

7.

8.

9.

My reality is a reflection of my choices.
What I desire is already present within me.

morning - 3   Date: /   /

1.

2.

3.

afternoon - 6

1.

2.

3.

4.

5.

6.

evening - 9   Date: /   /

1.

2.

3.

4.

5.

6.

7.

8.

9.

I am the originator of my own reality.
I deserve to live a life that is in alignment with my heart's desires.

morning - 3

Date: / /

1.

2.

3.

afternoon - 6

1.

2.

3.

4.

5.

6.

evening - 9   Date: /   /

1.

2.

3.

4.

5.

6.

7.

8.

9.

My perception creates my reality.
I am deserving of all the blessings that come my way.

morning - 3   Date: /   /

1.

2.

3.

afternoon - 6

1.

2.

3.

4.

5.

6.

evening - 9   Date: /   /

1.

2.

3.

4.

5.

6.

7.

8.

9.

I am the architect of my reality.
My desires reflect my authentic self.

morning - 3

Date: /   /

1.

2.

3.

afternoon - 6

1.

2.

3.

4.

5.

6.

evening - 9   Date: /   /

1.

2.

3.

4.

5.

6.

7.

8.

9.

My mindset and actions shape my reality.
I am open to receiving all that I deserve and more.

MANIFESTATION
takeaways

We hope this manifestation journal has helped you attract your desires. How did affirmations help you?

By working through this journal, how is life better, different or new?

Would you recommend this journal to a friend? What would you say?

Thank you for purchasing this journal! We hope it helped you manifest your desires and we hope continuing to journal brings great joy into your life.

www.ingramcontent.com/pod-product-compliance
Lightning Source LLC
Chambersburg PA
CBHW050305120526
44590CB00016B/2504